Mastering CCAT

Canadian Cognitive Abilities Test
CogAT Non-Verbal Reasoning
Grades 5-7

Includes:

- **Review of Non-Verbal Reasoning Types**
- **Timed Practice Tests with Answers**
- **Aligned with CCAT Curriculum**
- **Details about CCAT Exams**

Table of contents

Chapter 1: About CCAT Tests

The CCAT (Canadian Cognitive Abilities Test) is an assessment used in Canada to measure students' cognitive development and ability to reason. It helps identify students for gifted and talented programs and assesses how students learn and process information.

Key Information:

Grades: The CCAT is typically administered to students in Grades 1 to 8, though the specific grade range can vary depending on the school board.

Format: The test evaluates three main areas:

- **Verbal reasoning**: Understanding words and concepts.
- **Quantitative reasoning**: Solving math-related problems.
- **Non-verbal reasoning**: Solving problems using visual and spatial reasoning.

The test usually contains multiple-choice questions across these three sections.

Year/Version: Schools generally use different versions of the test, depending on the region and testing year, but the CCAT has several editions that are updated periodically.

This book focuses on non-verbal part of this test. CCAT non-verbal reasoning section is designed to assess a student's ability to think logically and solve complex, non-verbal problems. The non-verbal reasoning section evaluates how well students can recognize patterns, relationships, and sequences without relying on language or mathematical formulas.

Purpose of the test: Identifying cognitive abilities for school placement and gifted programs

General Format for non-verbal reasoning part:

Question Types

- Patterns and Sequences: Identifying and continuing patterns involving shapes, colors, and numbers.

- Symmetry and Rotations: Recognizing symmetrical shapes and understanding the effect of rotations.

- Logical Sequencing: Completing sequences based on logical rules or patterns.

- Analogies: Finding relationships between pairs of shapes or numbers and applying the same logic to another pair.

- Odd One Out: Identifying the item in a set that does not fit the given pattern or rule.

Number of Questions

There are typically **150 to 180 multiple-choice questions** in total, distributed evenly across the three sections verbal, non-verbal and quantitative reasoning.

Duration

As mentioned earlier, the CCAT is divided into 3 main sections: Verbal, Quantitative, and Non-verbal Reasoning. Each section is approximately 30-40 minutes, with a total testing time of 90-120 minutes.

Marking Scheme

- Each question usually has a single correct answer.

- There might be no negative marking for incorrect answers, but this can vary.

Question Format

- **Multiple Choice**: Most questions are in a multiple-choice format with 3-4 options.

- **Visual and Numerical**: Questions may include visual patterns or numerical sequences.

Test Date

Scheduling

The CCAT (Canadian Cognitive Abilities Test) does not have a standardized national schedule in Canada. The test is typically administered based on individual school boards or district schedules. However, most schools conduct the test during the following periods:

- Fall (September to November): Many schools schedule the test at the beginning of the academic year to assess students early and determine their placement in special programs like gifted and talented education.
- Spring (February to April): Some school boards opt to administer the test in the spring, giving students and teachers time to complete most of the curriculum.

You should check with the specific school board or school for the exact testing date for Grade 6.

Registration Deadlines

The CCAT (Canadian Cognitive Abilities Test) in Canada typically does not require direct registration by students or parents. Instead, it is usually administered by schools or school boards as part of their standard testing procedures. The process often works as follows:

- Automatic Registration: Schools or school boards generally handle registration for the CCAT. If the school has chosen to administer the test, students are automatically registered.
- Notification: Parents are typically notified by the school about the testing date, usually a few weeks or months in advance.

Steps for Parents:

1. Check with the School: Contact your child's school or school board to confirm if the CCAT will be administered for Grade 6 and when it is scheduled.
2. Gifted Program Applications: If the CCAT is being used as part of an application process for a gifted program, there might be separate deadlines to apply for the program itself, which could involve submission of forms, academic records, or teacher recommendations.

It's essential to reach out to your local school or school board for specific information regarding deadlines or testing windows.

General Rules

1. No Special Preparation Required: The CCAT is designed to assess a student's cognitive abilities, so there is no need for special content preparation (like subject-specific studying). However, practice in reasoning skills and test-taking strategies can be helpful.
2. No Calculators or Electronic Devices: Calculators, cell phones, and other electronic devices are not permitted during the test. Students must rely on mental calculations and reasoning.
3. Scratch Paper: Scratch paper is usually provided for rough work, especially for the Quantitative Reasoning section. However, answers must be marked on the answer sheet, not on the scratch paper.
4. Pencils and Erasers: Students should bring pencils (typically No. 2) and erasers, as they will need to fill in the answer bubbles clearly. No pens or mechanical pencils are allowed.
5. No Outside Help: Once the test begins, no external assistance is allowed. Teachers or proctors can clarify instructions, but they cannot help with specific questions or content.
6. Follow Instructions Carefully: It's important to listen to the proctor's instructions and follow them carefully. This includes when to start, how to fill out the answer sheet, and what to do if you need help with directions.
7. Skipping Questions: If a student is unsure of a question, they are encouraged to skip it and return to it later if time permits. There is usually no penalty for wrong answers (no negative marking), so students are encouraged to answer all questions.
8. Breaks: There may be short breaks between sections, depending on the test administration schedule, but no breaks during individual sections.

Test Results:

Results are typically provided to parents and teachers by the school or school board and are used to help identify students for gifted programs or to assess cognitive strengths and weaknesses.

Importance of Non verbal Reasoning Skills for Students

Non-verbal reasoning plays a significant role in a child's *cognitive development*. It enhances skills that are important not only for academic success but also for problem-solving in everyday life. Key benefits of non-verbal reasoning include:

- **Logical Thinking**: Developing the ability to approach problems in a structured, logical way.
- **Creative Problem**-Solving: Encouraging students to think outside the box and apply unique solutions.
- **Critical Analysis**: Strengthening the ability to break down complex information and identify key patterns or relationships.
- **Adaptability**: Equipping students with the skills needed to solve unfamiliar problems, a critical component in competitive exams like CCAT.

How to Use This Book Effectively

This book is designed to guide students through a systematic preparation for the CCAT non-verbal Reasoning Exam. Here's how to maximize its use:

- **Start with foundational concepts** – Begin by studying the basic principles of non verbal reasoning. These sections will introduce core concepts like pattern recognition, sequencing, and relationships.
- **Progress through increasing difficulty** – The book is structured so that each chapter builds on the last. Start with easier questions and work your way up to more complex problems as your skills improve.
- **Practice under exam conditions** – The book includes timed practice sections to simulate the actual exam environment. This helps build not only reasoning skills but also time management abilities.
- **Review thoroughly** – After completing exercises, go over any mistakes in detail. Use the step-by-step solutions provided to fully understand the logic behind each question.
- **Track progress and set goals** – Use each chapter's exercises and the full-length practice tests to measure your improvement. Set specific targets for accuracy and speed to challenge yourself.

By using this book consistently and methodically, students will be well-prepared to succeed in the CCAT Non-verbal Reasoning Exam, gaining confidence and mastering the skills needed for these highly competitive assessments.

Chapter 2: Understanding Non-Verbal Reasoning

Non verbal reasoning is a critical thinking skill that involves analyzing and solving problems that require non-verbal logic and pattern recognition. It requires students to:

- Identify relationships between shapes, figures, or patterns.
- Recognize sequences and progressions without relying on language or numerical calculations.
- Apply logical reasoning to figure out how shapes and patterns change and how they can be continued or completed.

In the context of the CCAT exam, non-verbal reasoning tests a student's ability to approach unfamiliar problems logically and find solutions by recognizing hidden relationships and rules governing sequences or patterns.

Types of Questions: Non-verbal reasoning questions generally fall into following categories:

1. **Patterns Completion**: These questions present a series of shapes, symbols, or objects that follow a certain rule or pattern. The task is to identify the rule and either complete the pattern or choose the next figure in the sequence.
   Example: You may be given a set of shapes that increase in size or change color systematically. You need to determine the pattern and select the next shape that fits.
2. **Sequences**: In these questions, students must find the logical progression in a series of figures, which may change based on size, rotation, shading, or position.
   Example: A series of arrows that rotate clockwise. The challenge is to predict how the next arrow will appear based on the pattern of rotation.
3. **Analogies**: These questions test the ability to understand relationships between different figures. One pair of figures will be related in a specific way, and the student must find a second pair that shares the same relationship.
   Example: "Figure A is to Figure B as Figure C is to ?". If Figure A is a triangle, and Figure B is a triangle rotated 90 degrees, you must determine what shape Figure D should be to correspond to Figure C in the same way.
4. **Spatial visualization:** Spatial visualization is the ability to mentally manipulate, rotate, twist, or invert objects in space. It involves understanding and remembering the spatial relationships between objects, which is crucial for solving problems that require recognizing patterns, predicting outcomes, and visualizing transformations.
   Example:
   - Identifying which rotated version of a shape matches a given figure.

- Finding the line of symmetry in a complex shape.
- Choosing the correct mirror image from multiple options.
- Determining how a 3D object looks from a different angle.

5. **Serial reasoning:** Serial reasoning involves identifying patterns and sequences in a series of objects, numbers, or shapes. It requires understanding the rule or logic behind how elements change or progress from one to the next. In tests like the CCAT, serial reasoning tests a student's ability to analyze sequential relationships, predict the next step in the series, and apply logical thinking. Serial reasoning questions typically involve:

   - **Numeric Series**: Identifying a pattern in a series of numbers and predicting the next number. Eg: 2, 4, 8, 16, _ ?   (Answer 32)

   - **Alphanumeric Series**: A combination of letters and numbers arranged in a logical sequence. A, C, F, J, _ ?   (Answer O)

   - **Geometric Series**: A progression of shapes or figures where students must identify changes in size, orientation, shading, or position.

     Square → 2. Triangle → 3. Pentagon → 4. Hexagon → _ ? (Answer heptagon)

   - **Progression of Symbols/Patterns**: A series of symbols that change according to a specific rule, such as rotation or the number of sides in a shape.

     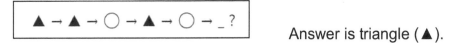   Answer is triangle (▲).

6. **Visual recognition:** Visual recognition in non-verbal reasoning refers to the ability to identify, differentiate, and match patterns or images based on their visual attributes. This includes recognizing similarities and differences in shapes, patterns, symbols, and figures. It is an essential skill in exams like the CCAT, where students are often required to spot visual patterns, complete figures, or identify the odd one out.

7. **Logical thinking word problems:** Logical thinking word problems assess a student's ability to apply reasoning skills to solve problems presented in a narrative format. These problems require students to interpret information, identify relevant details, and use logical steps to arrive at a solution

8. **Odd one out:** In this section, students have to extract the image or number that does not fit into the defined pattern of images or numbers

Key Strategies for Solving Non-verbal Reasoning Problems:

Success in non-verbal reasoning relies not only on recognizing patterns but also on using effective strategies to solve problems quickly and accurately. Here are some key approaches:

1. **Break Down the Question**: Look at each figure or pattern and identify individual elements (e.g., shapes, colors, directions). Analyze how each element changes from one figure to the next.
2. **Identify the Rule**: Determine the rule or set of rules that governs the progression of figures. Is it based on size, rotation, direction, or shading? Try to focus on the most obvious change first and then identify any secondary changes.
3. **Elimination Method**: When dealing with multiple-choice questions, eliminate options that clearly do not fit the pattern. This method helps narrow down the possibilities and makes it easier to identify the correct answer.
4. **Work Systematically**: Tackle each part of the problem in a step-by-step manner. For example, if a pattern involves both rotation and color change, analyze one factor at a time.
5. **Practice Speed and Accuracy**: Non-verbal reasoning tests are often timed, so it's important to practice solving problems quickly. However, don't sacrifice accuracy for speed. Begin by practicing slowly and carefully, then work on improving your speed over time.
6. **Stay Calm and Focused**: Sometimes patterns aren't immediately obvious. If you're stuck, take a moment to refocus and break the problem down again. Don't rush into guessing. Staying calm helps you think clearly and apply logical reasoning effectively.

By mastering these strategies and familiarizing yourself with the types of questions, you will be well-prepared for the non verbal reasoning section of the CCAT exam. Regular practice with a variety of patterns, sequences, and analogies will help you strengthen these essential problem-solving skills.

Chapter 3: Problem-Solving Strategies

Non verbal reasoning tests assess a student's ability to understand and analyze patterns, shapes, and logical relationships. Here are some effective strategies to help students excel in these tests:

1. **Understand the Question** Types: As discussed in previous chapters, understanding the questions format is first thing to ace the CCAT tests

    1. Pattern Recognition: Look for repetitive sequences or changes in shapes, colors, or numbers. Pay attention to the direction of patterns (e.g., increasing or decreasing).
    2. Symmetry and Rotations: Visualize how a shape looks when rotated or mirrored. Practice with shapes and figures to build familiarity.
    3. Logical Sequencing: Identify the rule governing the sequence (e.g., addition, subtraction). Apply the rule to find the missing element.
    4. Analogies Determine how the first pair of shapes or numbers relate to each other and apply that relationship to the second pair.
    5. Odd One Out: Compare each item with others to find the one that differs in a key attribute.

2. **Practice Regularly**

Use Practice Tests: Familiarize yourself with the test format and question types. Take timed practice tests to simulate the test environment and improve speed and accuracy. Review Mistakes: Learn from errors to avoid repeating them. After practice tests, review incorrect answers and understand why the correct answers are right.

3. **Develop Problem-Solving Skills**:

Simplify complex problems into manageable parts. Focus on one part of the problem at a time and solve it step by step.

Work Backwards: Verify solutions by reversing the process. If a problem is complex, start from the end and work backward to ensure the solution fits the given conditions.

4. **Enhance Visual and Logical Thinking**

Practice Visualization: Improve the ability to mentally manipulate shapes and patterns.

Use tools like pattern puzzles, shape manipulation games, and visual reasoning exercises.

Understand Common Patterns: Study common patterns and rules used in non-verbal reasoning tests, such as alternating sequences or geometric transformations.

5. Time Management

- Allocate Time Wisely: Divide the total time by the number of questions to allocate a reasonable amount of time for each. Adjust as needed based on question difficulty.
- Skip and Return: Skip difficult questions and return to them later if time permits. This ensures you maximize your score by addressing all easier questions first.

6. Stay Calm and Focused

- Practice Relaxation Techniques: Practice deep breathing, visualization, or other relaxation techniques before and during the test to reduce anxiety.
- Stay Positive: Approach each question with a positive attitude and avoid dwelling on difficult questions.

Example Strategies in Action

Pattern Recognition Example

- Question: Sequence: Square, Triangle, Square, Triangle, _?
- Strategy: Identify the alternating pattern. The next shape is a Square.

Symmetry and Rotation Example

- Question: Which shape is the same when rotated 180 degrees?
- Strategy: Visualize or draw the shape and its rotated version. Select the shape that matches after rotation.

Logical Sequencing Example

- Question: Sequence: 3, 6, 12, 24, _?
- Strategy: Identify the multiplication pattern (each number is multiplied by 2). The next number is 48.

By applying these strategies, students can improve their performance on the CCAT non-verbal reasoning tests. Regular practice and a focused approach will help in mastering the types of questions typically found in these exams.

Practice Tests

In the following section, you'll find practice worksheets designed to help you sharpen your non-verbal reasoning skills.

Each worksheet includes a section at the top where you can record the date, start time, end time, and your score.

To make the most of these worksheets:
1. **Timing**: Set a timer for each practice session to simulate test conditions.
   In the Real CCAT non-verbal reasoning Test, there are 45-50 questions to be done in 30 minutes.
   Try to spend 35-40 seconds on each question.
   So, for each of the following Practice test (10 questions set), try to set timer of 7 minutes or less.
2. **Review**: After completing each worksheet, review your answers and note any mistakes.

Solutions are provided at the end of the book for reference.

Dive in and enjoy the testing process!

Practice Test 1

Date	Start time	End Time	Score

In the following questions, identify the figure that completes the pattern

1. Complete the Pattern:

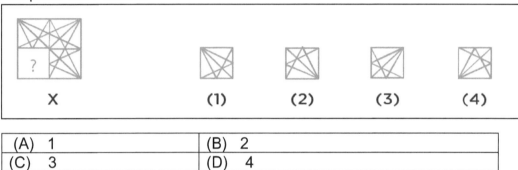

(A) 1	(B) 2
(C) 3	(D) 4

2. Complete the Pattern:

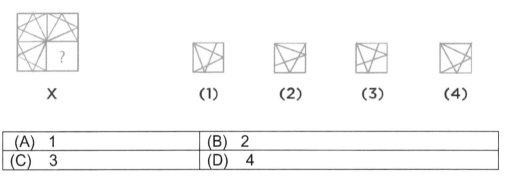

(A) 1	(B) 2
(C) 3	(D) 4

3. Complete the Pattern:

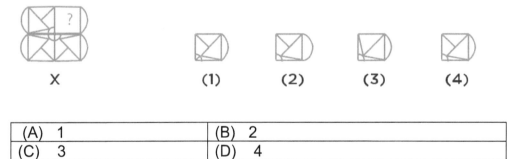

(A) 1	(B) 2
(C) 3	(D) 4

4. Complete the Pattern:

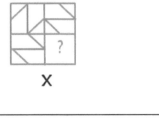

(1)	(2)	(3)	(4)

(A) 1	(B) 2
(C) 3	(D) 4

5. Complete the Pattern:

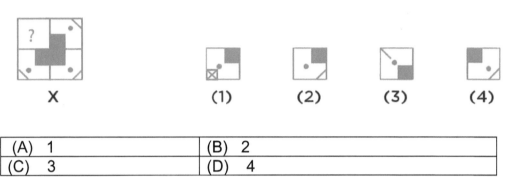

(A) 1	(B) 2
(C) 3	(D) 4

6. Complete the Pattern:

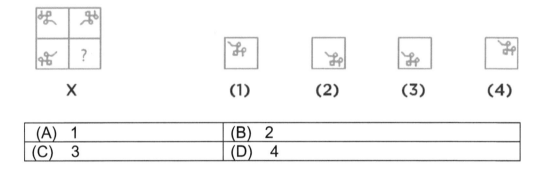

(A) 1	(B) 2
(C) 3	(D) 4

7. Complete the Pattern:

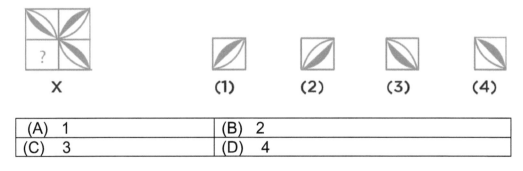

(A) 1	(B) 2
(C) 3	(D) 4

8. Complete the Pattern:

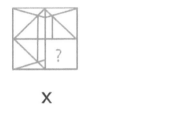

X   (1)   (2)   (3)   (4)

(A) 1	(B) 2
(C) 3	(D) 4

9. Complete the Pattern:

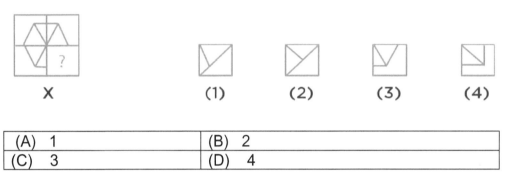

X   (1)   (2)   (3)   (4)

(A) 1	(B) 2
(C) 3	(D) 4

10. Complete the Pattern:

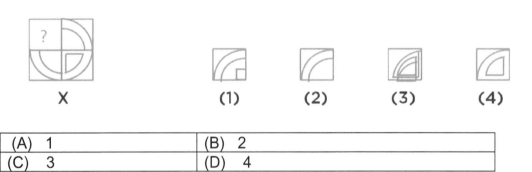

X   (1)   (2)   (3)   (4)

(A) 1	(B) 2
(C) 3	(D) 4

Practice Test 2

Date	Start time	End Time	Score

Serial Reasoning questions:

Select the option from the "Answer Figures" which will continue the same series as established by the five problem figures

1. What is the next figure in the series?

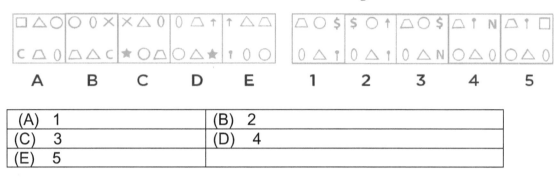

(A)	1	(B)	2
(C)	3	(D)	4
(E)	5		

2. What is the next figure in the series?

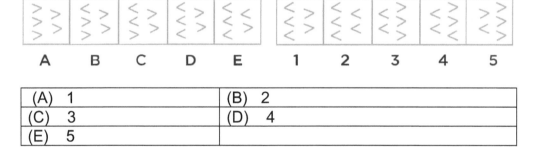

(A)	1	(B)	2
(C)	3	(D)	4
(E)	5		

3. What is the next figure in the series?

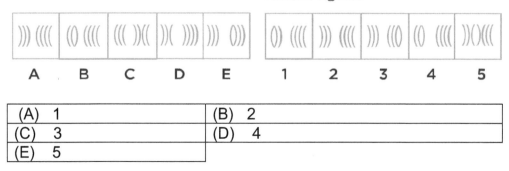

(A)	1	(B)	2
(C)	3	(D)	4
(E)	5		

4. What is the next figure in the series?

Answer figures

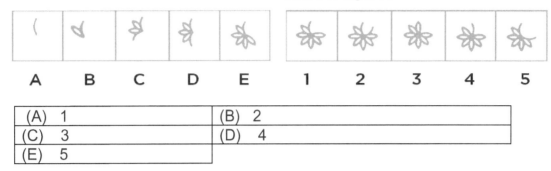

A	B	C	D	E	1	2	3	4	5

(A)	1	(B)	2
(C)	3	(D)	4
(E)	5		

5. What is the next figure in the series?

Answer figures

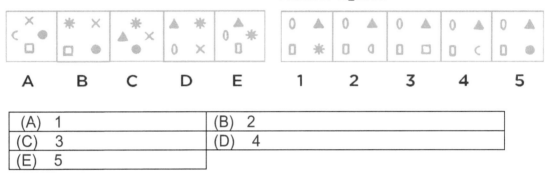

A	B	C	D	E	1	2	3	4	5

(A)	1	(B)	2
(C)	3	(D)	4
(E)	5		

6. What is the next figure in the series?

Answer figures

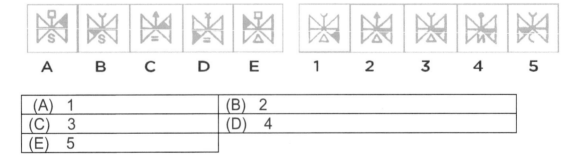

A	B	C	D	E	1	2	3	4	5

(A)	1	(B)	2
(C)	3	(D)	4
(E)	5		

7. What is the next figure in the series?

Answer figures

A	B	C	D	E	1	2	3	4	5

(A)	1		
(C)	3	(D)	4
(E)	5		

8. What is the next figure in the series?

Answer figures

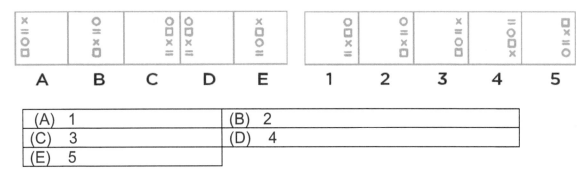

| A | B | C | D | E | 1 | 2 | 3 | 4 | 5 |

(A)	1	(B)	2
(C)	3	(D)	4
(E)	5		

9. What is the next figure in the series?

Answer figures

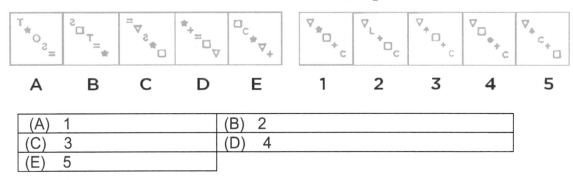

| A | B | C | D | E | 1 | 2 | 3 | 4 | 5 |

(A)	1	(B)	2
(C)	3	(D)	4
(E)	5		

10. What is the next figure in the series?

Answer figures

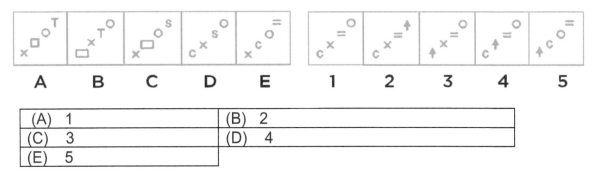

| A | B | C | D | E | 1 | 2 | 3 | 4 | 5 |

(A)	1	(B)	2
(C)	3	(D)	4
(E)	5		

Practice Test 3

Date	Start time	End Time	Score

Spatial Visualization:

Select the option that most closely resembles the mirror image of the given pattern.

1. Find the Pattern's mirror image

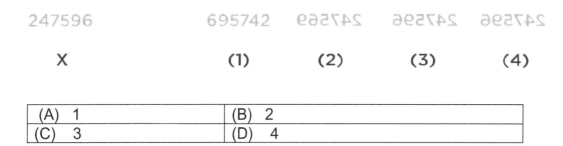

(A) 1	(B) 2
(C) 3	(D) 4

2. Find the Pattern's mirror image

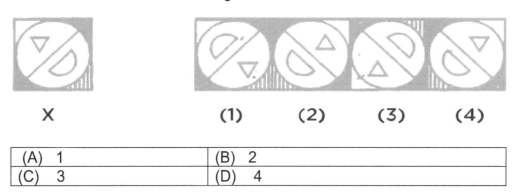

(A) 1	(B) 2
(C) 3	(D) 4

3. Find the Pattern's mirror image

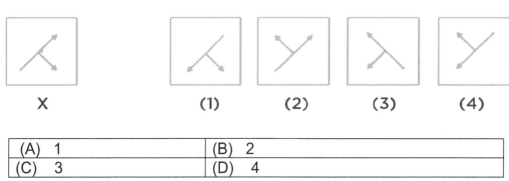

(A) 1	(B) 2
(C) 3	(D) 4

4. Find the Pattern's mirror image

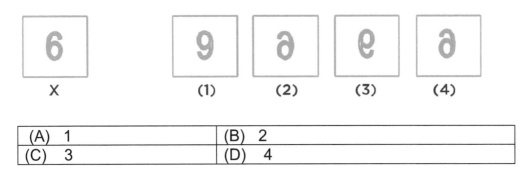

(A) 1	(B) 2
(C) 3	(D) 4

5. Find the Pattern's mirror image

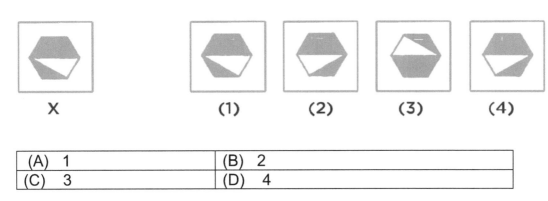

(A) 1	(B) 2
(C) 3	(D) 4

6. Find the Pattern's mirror image

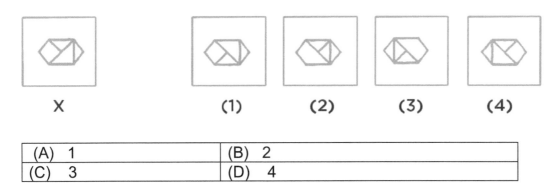

(A) 1	(B) 2
(C) 3	(D) 4

7. Pattern's unfolded form: Choose a figure which would resemble the unfolded form of figure Z

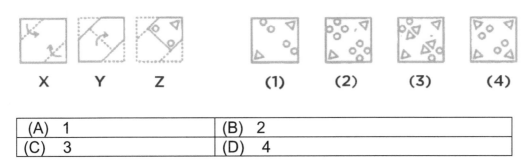

(A) 1	(B) 2
(C) 3	(D) 4

8. Pattern's unfolded form: Choose a figure which would resemble the unfolded form of figure Z

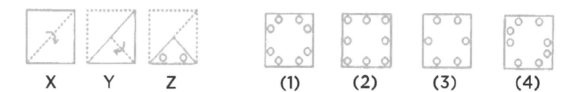

(A) 1	(B) 2
(C) 3	(D) 4

9. Pattern's mirror unfolded form: Choose a figure which would resemble the unfolded form of figure Z

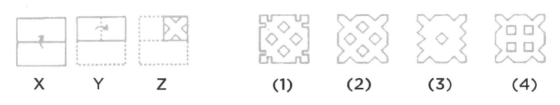

(A) 1	(B) 2
(C) 3	(D) 4

10. Find the Pattern's mirror image

(A) 1	(B) 2
(C) 3	(D) 4

Practice Test 4

Date	Start time	End Time	Score

Select the option that will complete the figure matrix

1. Complete the Matrix

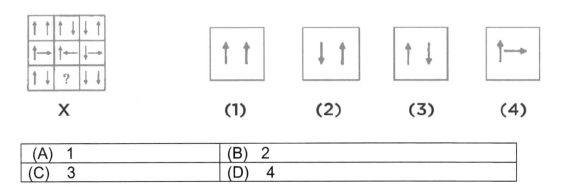

(A) 1	(B) 2
(C) 3	(D) 4

2. Complete the Matrix

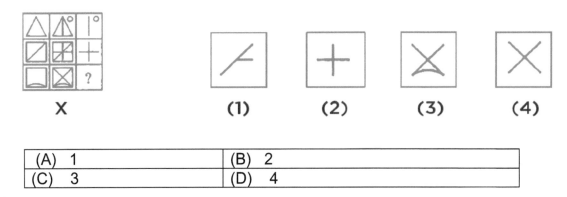

(A) 1	(B) 2
(C) 3	(D) 4

3. Complete the Matrix

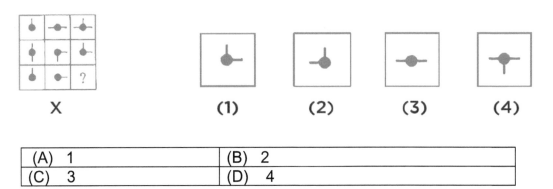

(A) 1	(B) 2
(C) 3	(D) 4

4. Complete the Matrix

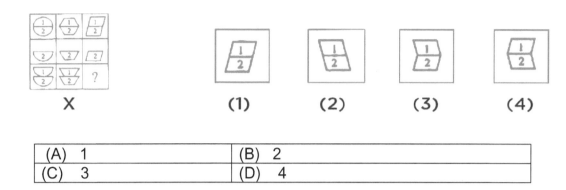

X   (1)   (2)   (3)   (4)

(A) 1	(B) 2
(C) 3	(D) 4

5. Complete the Matrix

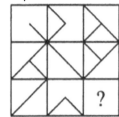
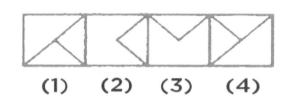

(1)   (2)   (3)   (4)

(A) 1	(B) 2
(C) 3	(D) 4

6. Complete the Matrix

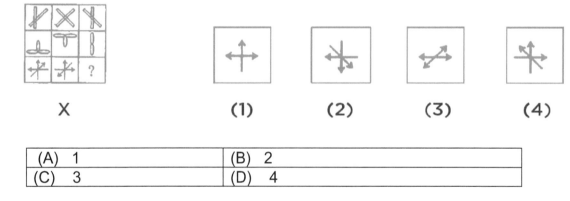

X   (1)   (2)   (3)   (4)

(A) 1	(B) 2
(C) 3	(D) 4

7. Complete the Matrix

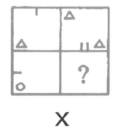
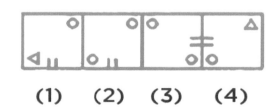

X   (1)   (2)   (3)   (4)

(A) 1	(B) 2
(C) 3	(D) 4

8. Complete the Matrix

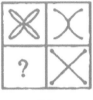

X

 (1)   (2)   (3)   (4)

(A) 1	(B) 2
(C) 3	(D) 4

9. Complete the Matrix

X

 (1)   (2)   (3)   (4)

(A) 1	(B) 2
(C) 3	(D) 4

10. Complete the Matrix

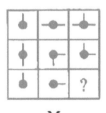

X

 (1)   (2)   (3)   (4)

(A) 1	(B) 2
(C) 3	(D) 4

Practice Test 5

Date	Start time	End Time	Score

Sequence Completion

1. Find the missing figure

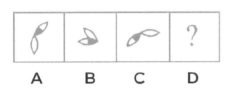

Answer figures

(A) 1	(B) 2
(C) 3	(D) 4
(E) 5	

2. Find the missing figure

Answer figures

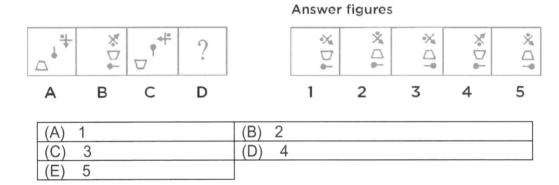

(A) 1	(B) 2
(C) 3	(D) 4
(E) 5	

3. Find the missing figure

Answer figures

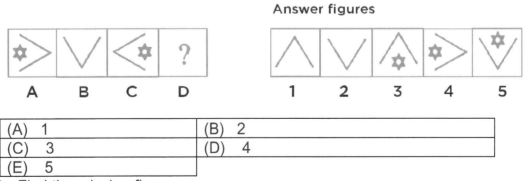

(A) 1	(B) 2
(C) 3	(D) 4
(E) 5	

4. Find the missing figure

A	B	C	D

(A)	1	(B)	2
(C)	3	(D)	4
(E)	5		

5. Find the missing figure

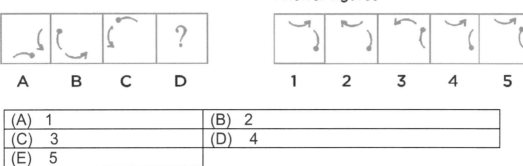

(A)	1	(B)	2
(C)	3	(D)	4
(E)	5		

6. Find the missing figure

Answer figures

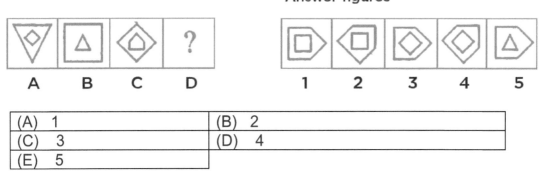

(A)	1	(B)	2
(C)	3	(D)	4
(E)	5		

7. Find the missing figure

Answer figures

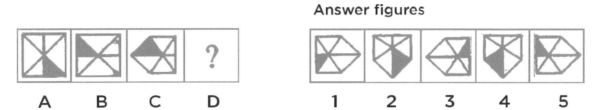

(A) 1	(B) 2
(C) 3	(D) 4
(E) 5	

8. Find the missing figure

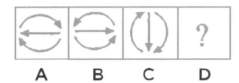

A   B   C   D

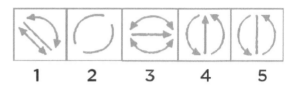

1   2   3   4   5

(A) 1	(B) 2
(C) 3	(D) 4
(E) 5	

9. Find the missing figure

Answer figures

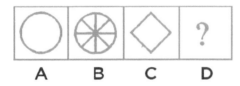

A   B   C   D

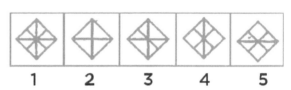

1   2   3   4   5

(A) 1	(B) 2
(C) 3	(D) 4
(E) 5	

10. Find the missing figure

Answer figures

A   B   C   D

1   2   3   4   5

(A) 1	(B) 2
(C) 3	(D) 4
(E) 5	

Practice Test 6

Date	Start time	End Time	Score

Logical thinking:

1. Look at the picture and answer the questions belo

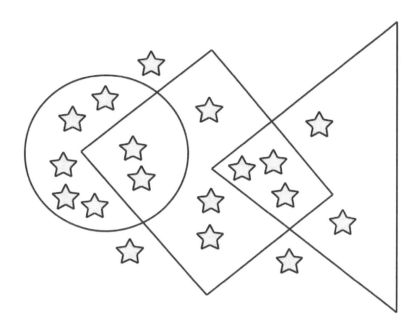

Number of Stars, only in the circle	
Number of Stars, only in the square	
Number of Stars, only in the triangle	
Number of Stars, in both circle and the square	
Number of Stars, in both square and the triangle	
Number of Stars, in neither the circle nor the triangle	
Number of Stars, not in any of the shapes Total number of Stars	

2. Look at the picture and answer the questions below

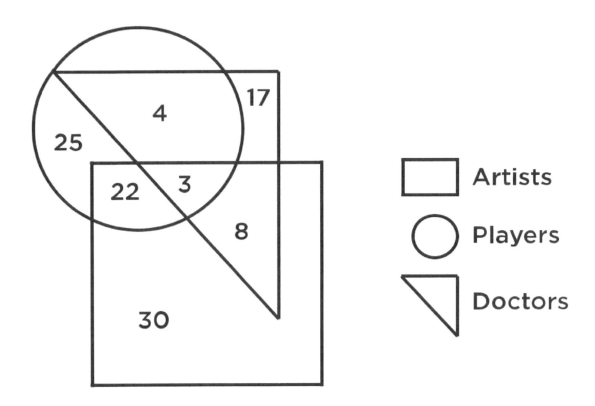

How many doctors are neither artists nor players ?

How many doctors are both players and artists ?

How many artists are players ?

How many players are neither artists nor doctors ?

How many artists are neither players nor doctors ?

3. Look at the picture and answer the questions below

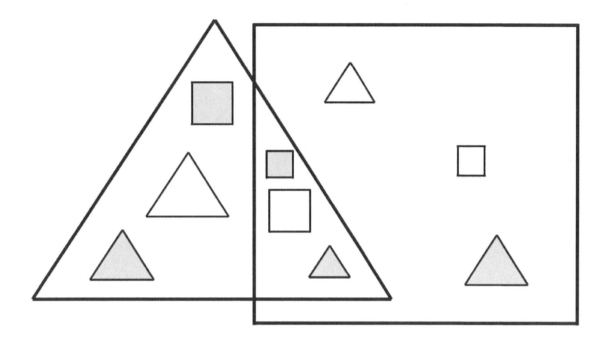

Triangles in big triangle

Squares in big squares

Triangles in big triangle only

Squares in big squares only

Squares in both big shapes

Triangles in both big shapes

Triangles in Big square only

Squares in big triangle only

4. Look at the picture and answer the questions below

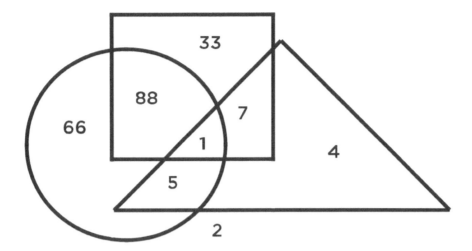

Which numbers are in either triangle or the square	
Which numbers are in both the triangle and the square	
Which numbers are in both the square and the circle	
Which numbers are in either circle or the triangle	
Which numbers are in all the three shapes	
Which numbers are not in any shape	
Which numbers are in neither the circle, not the triangle	
Which numbers are in neither the circle nor the square	

5. Look at the picture and answer the questions below

♡	♡		♡	
♡		♡		♡
♡	♡		♡	
		♡		♡

How many hearts are not in the top row?	
How many hearts are not in the bottom row?	
How many hearts are not in the middle two rows?	
How many hearts are not in the top two rows?	
How many hearts are there in all?	
How many blank spaces are there in all?	

Practice Test 7

Date	Start time	End Time	Score

Visual Recognition:

In the following questions, choose the odd one out that is find out the image that is different from the rest of the images

   1. Find the Odd one out

(A) 1	(B) 2
(C) 3	(D) 4
(E) 5	

   2. Find the Odd one out

(A) 1	(B) 2
(C) 3	(D) 4
(E) 5	

   3. Find the Odd one out

(A) 1	(B) 2
(C) 3	(D) 4
(E) 5	

4. Find the Odd one out

(A) 1	(B) 2
(C) 3	(D) 4
(E) 5	

5. Find the Odd one out

(A) 1	(B) 2
(C) 3	(D) 4
(E) 5	

6. Find the Odd one out

(A) 1	(B) 2
(C) 3	(D) 4
(E) 5	

7. Find the Odd one out

(A)	1	(B)	2
(C)	3	(D)	4
(E)	5		

8. Find the Odd one out

(A)	1	(B)	2
(C)	3	(D)	4
(E)	5		

9. Find the Odd one out

(A)	1	(B)	2
(C)	3	(D)	4
(E)	5		

10. Find the Odd one out

(A)	1	(B)	2
(C)	3	(D)	4
(E)	5		

Practice Test 8

Date	Start time	End Time	Score

Logical thinking word problems:

Question 1:

Fact 1: All boys like to run.
Fact 2: Some boys like to swim.
Fact 3: Some boys look like their dads.

If the first three statements are facts, which of the following statements must also be a fact?
I: All boys who like to swim look like their dads.
II: boys who like to swim also like to run.
III: boys who like to run do not look like their dads.

A:	I only	B:	II only
C:	II and III only	D:	None of the statements is a known fact.

Question 2:

Fact 1: Martha has four children
Fact 2: Two of the children have blue eyes and two of the children have brown eyes.
Fact 3: Half of the children are girls.

If the first three statements are facts, which of the following statements must also be a fact?
I: At least one girl has blue eyes.
II: To of the children are boys.
III:The boys have brown eyes.

A:	I only	B:	II only
C:	II and III only	D:	None of the statements is a known fact.

Question 3:

Fact 1:Most stuffed toys are stuffed with cotton.
Fact 2:There are stuffed bears and stuffed lions.
Fact 3:Some sofas are stuffed with cotton.

If the first three statements are facts, which of the following statements must also be a fact?
I:Only children's sofa are stuffed with cotton.
II:All stuffed lions are stuffed with cotton.
III:Stuffed monkeys are not stuffed with cotton.

A:	I only	B:	II only
C:	II and III only	D:	None of the statements is a known fact.

Question 4:

Fact 1:Maryln said, "Anny and I both have cats."
Fact 2:Anny said, "I don't have a cat."
Fact 3:Maryln always tells the truth, but Anny sometimes lies.

If the first three statements are facts, which of the following statements must also be a fact?
I:Anny has a cat.
II:Maryln has a cat.
III:Anny is lying.

A:	I only	B:	II only
C:	II and III only	D:	None of the statements is a known fact.

Question 5:

Fact 1: Rob has four vehicles.
Fact 2: Two of the vehicles are Blue.
Fact 3: One of the vehicles is a minivan.

If the first three statements are facts, which of the following statements must also be a fact?
I: Rob has a red minivan.
II: Rob has three cars.
III: Rob's favorite color is Blue.

A: I only	B: II only
C: II and III only	D: None of the statements is a known fact.

Practice Test 9

Date	Start time	End Time	Score

Mixed questions Non verbal reasoning:

1. What is next in the series

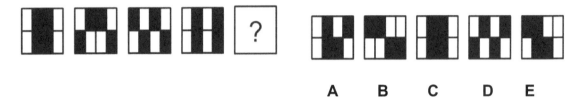

A   B   C   D   E

2. Select the odd one out

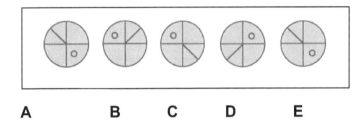

A   B   C   D   E

3. Select the option that completes the matrix

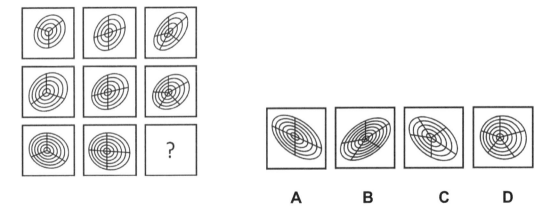

A   B   C   D

4. What is next in the series

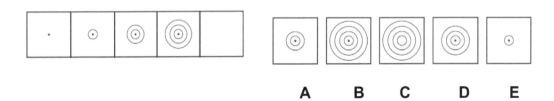

A   B   C   D   E

5. What is next in the series

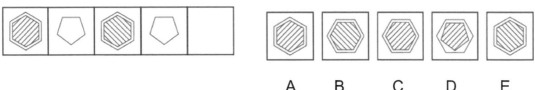

      A   B   C   D   E

6. What is the next in the series

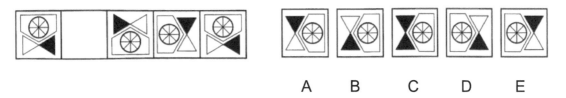

      A   B   C   D   E

7. What is the missing part in the series

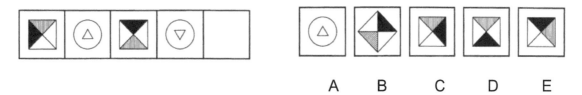

      A   B   C   D   E

8. What is the next in the series

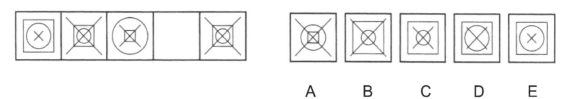

      A   B   C   D   E

9. What is the missing part in the series

10. What is the missing part in the series

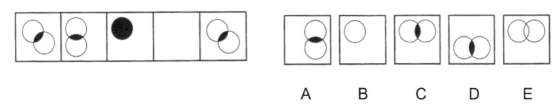

      A   B   C   D   E

Practice Test 10

Date	Start time	End Time	Score

1. In the following problems, a square transparent sheet with a pattern is given. Figure out from amongst the four alternatives how the pattern would appear when the transparent sheet is folded at the dotted line.

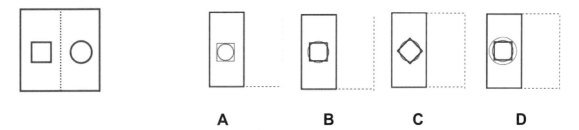

              A   **B**   **C**   **D**

2. In the following problems, a square transparent sheet with a pattern is given. Figure out from amongst the four alternatives how the pattern would appear when the transparent sheet is folded at the dotted line.

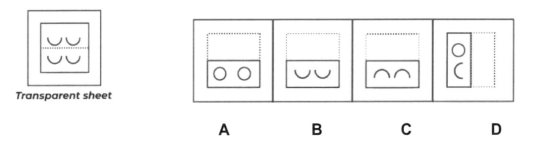

Transparent sheet

              A   **B**   **C**   **D**

3. Find out from among the four alternatives how the pattern would appear when the transparent sheet is folded at the dotted line.

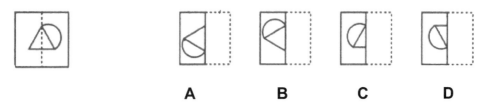

              A   **B**   **C**   **D**

4. Find out from among the four alternatives how the pattern would appear when the transparent sheet is folded at the dotted line.

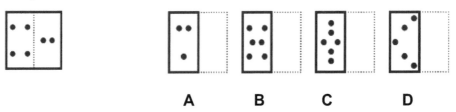

              A   **B**   **C**   **D**

5. Find out from among the four alternatives how the pattern would appear when the transparent sheet is folded at the dotted line.

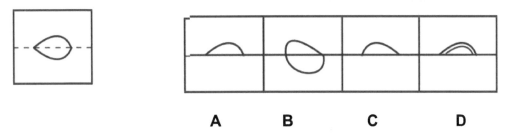

A   B   C   D

6. A sheet has been folded in the manner as shown in X, Y, and Z respectively, and punched. You have to choose from the alternatives how it will look when unfolded.

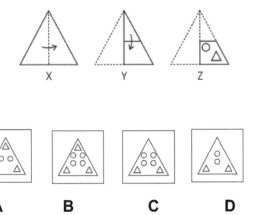

A   B   C   D

7. Find out from amongst the four alternatives how the pattern would appear when the transparent sheet is folded at the dotted line.

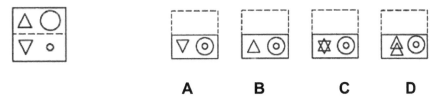

A   B   C   D

8. In the following problems, a square transparent sheet with a pattern is given. Figure out from amongst the four alternatives how the pattern would appear when the transparent sheet is folded at the dotted line.

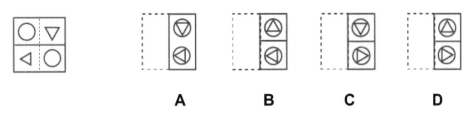

A   B   C   D

9. In the following problems, a square transparent sheet with a pattern is given. Figure out from amongst the four alternatives how the pattern would appear when the transparent sheet is folded at the dotted line.

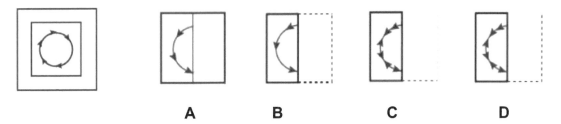

A   B   C   D

10. In the following problems, a square transparent sheet with a pattern is given. Figure out from amongst the four alternatives how the pattern would appear when the transparent sheet is folded at the dotted line.

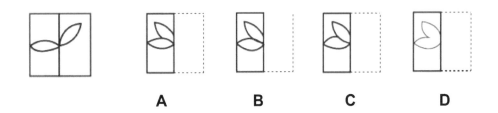

A   B   C   D

Practice Test 11

Date	Start time	End Time	Score

1. Which letter comes next in the series: **A, C, E, G, __?**

(A) I	(B) H
(C) F	(D) K

2. Which letter is missing in the series: **B, D, F, H, __, L?**

(A) K	(B) M
(C) N	(D) L

3. Which letter is missing in the series: **A, C, E, G, __, K.**

(A) I	(B) J
(C) H	(D) L

4. What symbol comes next: ***, $$, ***, $$$$$, __?**

(A) *****	(B) ****
(C) ******	(D) $$$$$$

5. Which letter is missing in the series **B, F, J, N, __, V.**

(A) Q	(B) T
(C) R	(D) S

6. Which letter **is missing in the series: Z, X, V, __, T, R?**

(A) P	(B) S
(C) Q	(D) U

7. Find the missing letters set in: **SCD, TEF, UGH, ___, WKL**

(A) CMN	(B) UJI
(C) VIJ	(D) IJT

8. Find the missing letters set in: **B2CD, ____, BCD4, B5CD, BC6D**

(A) B2C2D	(B) BC3D
(C) B2C3D	(D) BCD7

9. Find the missing letters set in: **ACE, GIK, MOQ, ___, UYK**

(A) ACG	(B) WSK
(C) EIS	(D) OPS

10. Find the missing letters set in: **KLM, NOP, QRQ, TUT, ___**

(A) WVW	(B) XYZ
(C) YZY	(D) ABC

Practice Test 12

Date	Start time	End Time	Score

Number Series

1. Given a Series 50, 45, 40, 35, 30, ?
   Find what number would come in place of the question mark(?).

(A) 28	(B) 15
(C) 25	(D) 20

2. Given a Series -10, -8, 6, 40, 102, ?
   Find what number would come in place of the question mark(?).

(A) 105	(B) 200
(C) 216	(D) 129

3. Given a Series 25,49,121,169,?
   Find what number would come in place of the question mark(?).

(A) 225	(B) 256
(C) 289	(D) 361

4. Given a Series 25,49,121,169,?
   Find what number would come in place of the question mark(?).

(A) 33	(B) 40
(C) 38	(D) 81

5. Given a Series 2, 3, 12, 37, 86, 166, 288.
   Find what number would come in place of the question mark(?).

(A) 25	(B) 49
(C) 27	(D) 64

6. Given a Series 2, 3, 12, 37, 86, 166, 288.
   Find what number which is wrong in this series?

(A) 2	(B) 12
(C) 37	(D) 166

7. Given a Series 3, 4, 7, 8, 11, 12, ?, ?.
   Find what number would come in place of the question mark(?).

(A) 13, 14	(B) 18, 20
(C) 15, 16	(D) 19, 20

8. Given a Series 14, 25, 47, 91, 179, ?.
   Find what number would come in place of the question mark(?).

(A) 255	(B) 321
(C) 355	(D) 211

9. Given a Series 4, 6, 9, 14, 21, ?.
   Find what number would come in place of the question mark(?).

(A) 28	(B) 32
(C) 34	(D) 40

10. Given a Series 1, 30 5, 26, 9, 22, 13, 18, ?
    Find what number would come in place of the question mark(?).

(A) 17	(B) 22
(C) 28	(D) 19

Practice Test 13

Date	Start time	End Time	Score

1. How many dots lie opposite to the face having three dots, when the given figure is folded to form a cube?

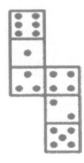

(A) 2	(B) 4
(C) 5	(D) 6

2. What is the example of a standard dice?

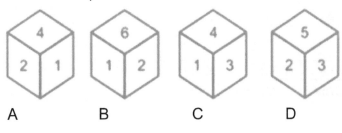

A   B   C   D

(A) A	(B) B
(C) C	(D) D

3. What is the opposite face of "Red"?

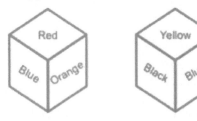

(A) Red	(B) Blue
(C) Yellow	(D) Black

4. Choose the box that is similar to the box formed from the given sheet of paper (X).

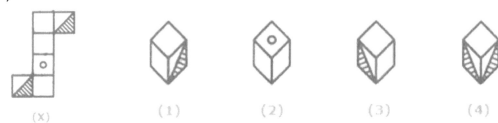

(A) 1 and 3 only	(B) 1 and 4 only
(C) 2 and 4 only	(D) 3 and 4 only

5. Choose the box that is similar to the box formed from the given sheet of paper (X).

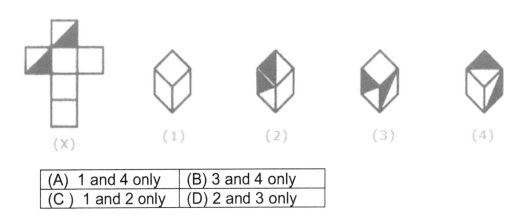

(A) 1 and 4 only	(B) 3 and 4 only
(C) 1 and 2 only	(D) 2 and 3 only

6. Two positions of a dice are shown below. Which number will appear on the face opposite to the face with the number 5?

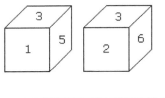

(A) 1	(B) 2
(C) 6	(D) 4

7. Two positions of dice are shown below. How many points will appear on the opposite to the face containing 5 points?

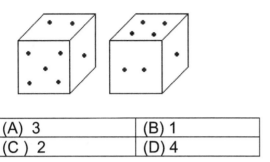

(A) 3	(B) 1
(C) 2	(D) 4

8. Two positions of a cube with its surfaces numbered are shown below. When the surface 4 touch the bottom, what surface will be on the top?

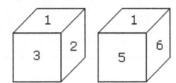

(A) 1	(B) 2
(C) 5	(D) 6

9. Two positions of dice are shown below. How many points will be on the top when 2 points are at the bottom?

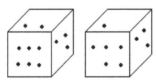

(A) 6	(B) 5
(C) 4	(D) 1

10. Here 4 positions of a cube are shown. Which sign will be opposite to '+' ?

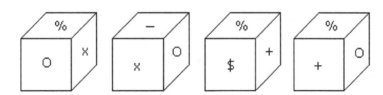

(A) %	(B) -
(C) x	(D) $

Practice Test 14

Date	Start time	End Time	Score

Mirror images and Water Images.

1. In the problem given below, try finding out the water image of the word **'RADIANT'**

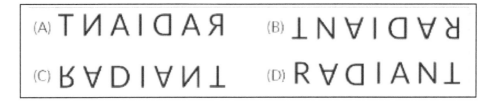

2. In the given problem, identify the correct mirror image of the following:
    C 6 8 D L A E A P E A

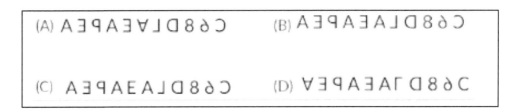

3. Identify the water image of the given object

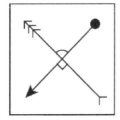

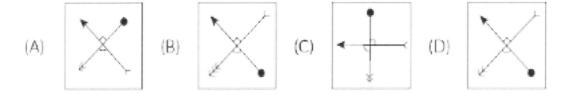

4. Identify the water image of the **block**

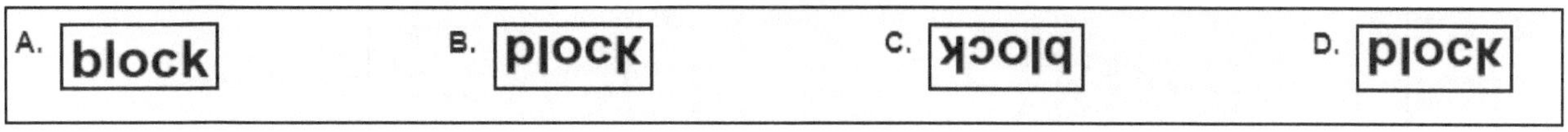

5. Identify the correct mirror image of the figure for the following combination of letters and numbers if the mirror is placed along the line MN.

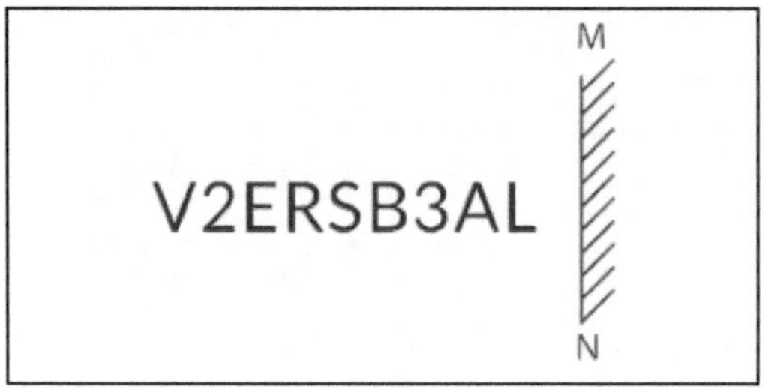

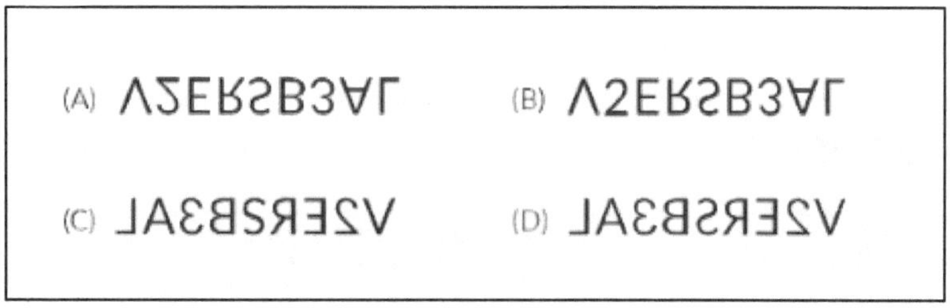

6. Identify the mirror image of the given figure if the mirror is placed vertically to the left of the figure.

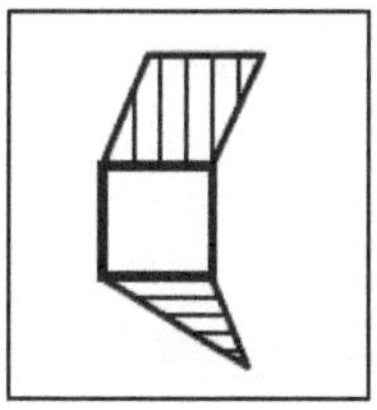

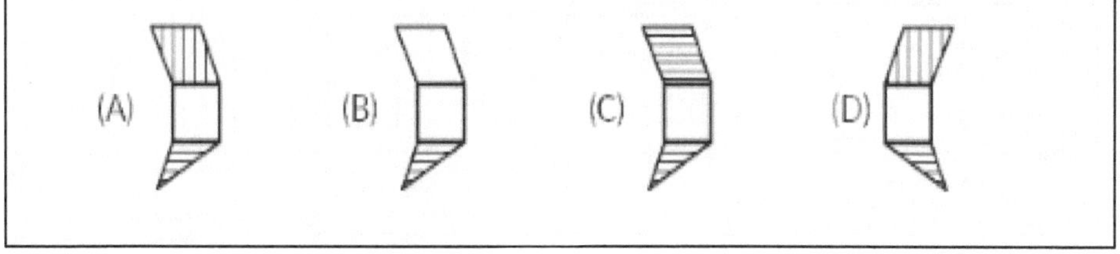

7. Identify the reflection of the given image, if the mirror is placed exactly vertical to the right of the given image

57BDE4

(A) 57BDE4   (B) 57BDE4

(C) 57BDE4   (D) 57BDE4

8. Choose the alternative which is closely resembles the water-image of the given combination. **NUCLEAR**

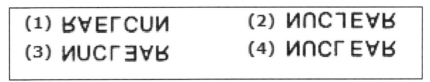

(A) 1	(B) 2
(C) 3	(D) 4

9. Choose the alternative which is closely resembles the water-image of the given combination. **A1M3b**

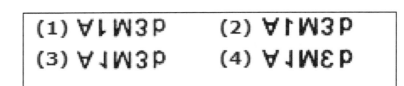

(A) 1	(B) 2
(C) 3	(D) 4

10. Choose the correct mirror image of the given figure (X) from amongst the four alternatives.

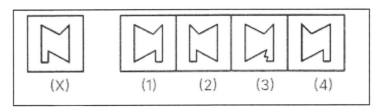

(A) 1	(B) 2
(C) 3	(D) 4

Practice Test 15

Date	Start time	End Time	Score

Odd One Out:

1. Look at the given figures and find the odd one out. Circle the correct option.

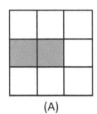 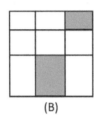 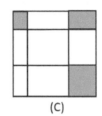 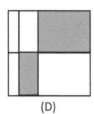

    (A)   (B)   (C)   (D)

2. Look at the given figures and find the odd one out. Choose the correct option.

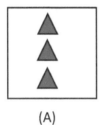 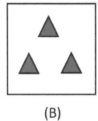 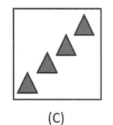 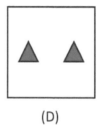

    (A)   (B)   (C)   (D)

3. Look at the given figures and find the odd one out. Choose the correct option.

 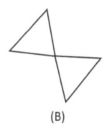 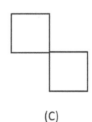 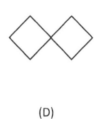

    (A)   (B)   (C)   (D)

4. Look at the given figures and find the odd one out. Choose the correct option.

 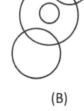  

    (A)   (B)   (C)   (D)

5. Look at the given figures and find the odd one out. Choose the correct option.

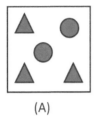 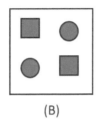 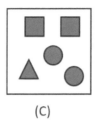 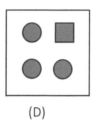

(A)   (B)   (C)   (D)

6. Look at the given figures and find the odd one out. Choose the correct option.

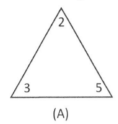 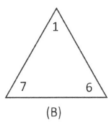 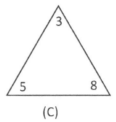 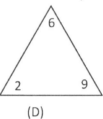

(A)   (B)   (C)   (D)

7. Look at the given figures and find the odd one out. Choose the correct option.

   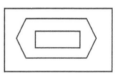

(A)   (B)   (C)   (D)

8. Look at the given figures and find the odd one out. Choose the correct option.

E   C   F   A

(A)   (B)   (C)   (D)

9. Look at the given figures and find the odd one out. Choose the correct option.

(A)   (B)   (C)   (D)

10. Look at the given figures and find the odd one out. Choose the correct option.

(A)

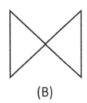

(B)

(C)

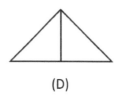

(D)

ANSWERS

Practice Test-1	Practice Test-2	Practice Test-3	Practice Test-4	Practice Test-5
1. D	1. A	1. D.	1. A.	1. C.
2. D	2. B	2. D.	2. D.	2. C.
3. D	3. B	3. C	3. A	3. A
4. A	4. A	4. B	4. C	4. C
5. D	5. B	5. D	5. B	5. D
6. B	6. C	6. D	6. C	6. D
7. B	7. E	7. B	7. C	7. B
8. B	8. C	8. A	8. C	8. D
9. C	9. C	9. B	9. B	9. A
10. D	10. C	10. D	10. A	10. A

Practice Test-6				
Question 1	Question 2	Question 3	Question 4	Question 5
1. 5	1. 17.	1. 3.	1. 1, 33,4,5,7,88	1. 8.
2. 6	2. 3	2. 3	2. 1,7	2. 9
3. 2	3. 25	3. 2	3. 1,88	3. 5
4. 2	4. 25	4. 1	4. 1,4,5,66,7,88	4. 5
5. 3	5. 30	5. 2	5. 1	5. 11
6. 6		6. 1	6. 2	6. 9
7. 3		7. 2	7. 2,3	
8. 18		8. 1	8. 2,4	

Practice Test-7	Practice Test-8	Practice Test-9	Practice Test-10
1. A.	1. B.	1. C.	1. B
2. A.	2. B.	2. B	2. A
3. C	3. D	3. D	3. B
4. C	4. D	4. B	4. B
5. C	5. D	5. C	5. A
6. C		6. A	6. A
7. A		7. B	7. C
8. D		8. C	8. C
9. A		9. E	9. C
10. C		10. C	10. B

Practice Test 11	Practice Test-12	Practice Test-13	Practice Test-14	Practice Test-15
1. A	1. C.	1. D	1. C	1. C.
2. C.	2. B.	2. A.	2. B	2. B.
3. C	3. C	3. C	3. B	3. A
4. D	4. C	4. A	4. B	4. A
5. B	5. A	5. A	5. D	5. C
6. D	6. D	6. C	6. A	6. D
7. C	7. C	7. D	7. D	7. C
8. C	8. C	8. A	8. D	8. A
9. B	9. B	9. D	9. C	9. D
10. A	10. A	10. C	10. D	10. B

Author's Message:

Dear Readers,

Congratulations on reaching the end of this book! You've journeyed through a variety of challenging and engaging non-verbal reasoning exercises, and I hope you've gained valuable skills and confidence along the way.

Non-verbal reasoning is not just about answering test questions—it's about learning to approach problems with a clear mind, recognize patterns, and think critically. These are skills that will serve you well, not only in exams but in many areas of life. I encourage you to continue practicing and applying what you've learned, as reasoning skills grow stronger with time and effort.

Thank you for choosing this book as part of your preparation. I hope it has been a helpful and rewarding resource.

Wishing you success in your upcoming exams and beyond!

Best regards,

Lucky. S.

> The function of education is to teach one to think intensively and to think critically. Intelligence plus character - that is the goal of true education.
>
> — *Martin Luther King* —